# BRITAIN
## IN COLOR

NEW YORK

In the days when the power of the Roman legions straddled this land, through present day England, Wales and parts of Scotland, they called the portion of the island they occupied *Britannia*.

England, the home of the Mother of Parliaments and a "green and pleasant land", has a wealth of scenery to delight the eye. There are the mountains and tarns of the Lake District; the windswept moors of the Pennines; the rolling Yorkshire Dales; the sleepy Cotswold villages, unchanged with time; the warm seashores of Cornwall, washed by the Gulf Stream; the bustling capital of London with the mighty River Thames at its heart; prehistoric Stonehenge standing on the sweep of Salisbury Plain; historic towns and cities like York; the cries of birds echoing over the desolate Fens of East Anglia; farmers ploughing their hedgerow-lined fields, and dry-stone walls which march over the uplands.

The immense variety of vistas almost seems to take the traveller unawares. Who would think that this relatively small country could contain such diversity? Leave behind the busy thoroughfares of any crowded town and you can see the undulating countryside before you; golden corn sways in the summer breezes under a blue sky containing ever-changing patterns of clouds; dense copses of trees stand silent with the weight of years; lambs dance sprightly in fields of verdure; rivers and streams wend their ways to the sea, which is sometimes calm and restful, but often displays the fierce force of turbulent nature as waves pound the nation's sea-girt walls.

Scotland is a majestic country of rugged beauty, with a turbulent history as its people fought to maintain their clan heritage and identity. For Sir Walter Scott it was the...

> "Land of brown heath and shaggy wood;
> Land of the mountain and the flood!"

It is also a country of jewel-like lochs; towering, scented conifers; bracken-covered moors; finest malt whiskies; castle strongholds; golf courses of international renown and a special kind of people. The landscapes are of a particularly wild and natural beauty, interwoven with a melancholic sense of history and strife. There have been heroes made of such men as Robert the Bruce and Sir William Wallace, both doughty fighters against the English Sassenachs. There were bloody battles fought at Bannockburn and Culloden, and there was defeat when the Scottish came south to Flodden Field:

> "Dool and wae for the order, sent our lads to the Border!
> The English, for ance, by guile wan the day;
> The Flowers of the Forest, that fought aye the foremost,
> The prime of our land, are cauld in the clay." (Jean Elliot)

There are still many places here in Scotland that have not been changed by the hand of time – Glencoe broods with an air of menace where the Macdonalds were slain by their treacherous guests.

The islands dotted around its coasts are places of enchantment, repositories of ancient culture and myth. It is a proud nation, now enjoying increasing prosperity with the advent of the North Sea oil industry.

Wales is a mountainous country, divided by beautiful valleys, and crystal streams and rivers including the Severn, Clwyd, Conway and Usk. It is blessed with wonderful scenery along the rugged Pembrokeshire coast; the magnificent Snowdonia National Park or the glacier-scoured hills of the Brecon Beacons. It is a land of legend, where King Arthur's wizard, Merlin, lived in his crystal cave. He was the child of a wizard and a princess, gifted with prophecy, becoming a prominent personage at the court of King Arthur, where his wealth of knowledge was much sought after. Wales is also a country which has produced great singers and fine poets, such as Dylan Thomas:

> "All the sun long it was running, it was lovely, the hay-
> Fields high as the house, the tunes from the chimneys, it was air
> And playing, lovely and watery
> And fire green as grass."

Much of the varied and historic attractions of colourful Britain lie around the next corner! It was J.B. Priestley who said that, "it would not surprise me if somebody decided to follow some tiny overgrown lane and then found that at the end of it Camelot was still there, with nettles thick around a dusty Round Table."

(Opposite page) Naunton, in the Cotswolds.

Buttressed battlements (opposite page) stand silhouetted by the golden glow of sun over still waters at Conwy Castle, Gwynedd. Harlech Castle (top right) was completed by Edward I in the 13th century. Conwy Castle (left) with a suspension bridge by Telford. Welsh legend holds that Constantine, Emperor of Constantinople, was born at Caernarvon Castle (top left). In 1969, Prince Charles was invested here by the Queen, as Prince of Wales (above).

"Among our ancient mountains,
And from our lovely vales,
Oh, let the prayer re-echo:
'God bless the Prince of Wales!'"

(George Linley)

The Pool and Craig Ddu (opposite page) seen from the mountain road to Aberystwyth. At Tal-y-llyn (top left) a cerulean hue suffuses the vista. A shepherd (top right) uses his dog to drive his sheep along a pluvial path at Dolgoch, near Towyn, deep in the mountain country of Cader Idris. Benlech (above) on the east coast of Anglesey. Waterfall in the Brecon Beacons (right) – "A sunny pleasure-dome with caves of ice!" (Coleridge)

Aberaeron (above) and Cardiff City Hall (right). St David's Cathedral (opposite page, top) and the longest station sign in Britain (opposite page, below). "There's no looking at a building here after seeing Italy" (Burney), but unique Portmeirion (below) is inspired by an Italian village.

LLANFAIRPWLLGWYNGYLLGOGERYCHWYRNDROBWYLL-LLANTYSILIOGOGOGOCH
RAILWAY STATION

Picturesque Polperro in Cornwall (opposite page). Newquay (right) is a leading resort of the South-West. Longships Lighthouse perches on a lonely Atlantic rock (below). St Michael's Mount (above) is part of King Arthur's lost kingdom of Lyonnesse.

"The rime was on the spray,
And starlight lit my lonesomeness
When I set out for Lyonnesse". (Hardy)

Sidmouth (opposite page, below) is bordered by spectacular cliffs. Clovelly (left) is one of the finest villages in Devon, with a steep main street. Widecombe-in-the-Moor (top) has a church dating from c1500, with a high, pinnacled tower introduced by tin-miners manifesting their newly acquired wealth. One of the charms of villages in Britain is their quaint thatched roofs, which can be seen at Buckland-in-the-Moor (above) and Bickleigh (opposite page, top).

"If I ever become a rich man,
Or if ever I grow to be old,
I will build a house with deep thatch
To shelter me from the cold". (Belloc)

The Clifton Suspension Bridge (top) was built by Brunel in 1864, spanning the River Avon where it flows between steep cliffs of limestone. Wells Cathedral, Somerset (left), was begun in the 12th century. Its west front was originally embellished with nearly 400 statues of saints, prophets and angels. The remains of Glastonbury Abbey (above). Florentine, shop-lined Pulteney Bridge in Bath (centre left) and the Abbey (opposite page) which has dominated the city, albeit in different form, since Saxon times. "Oh! who can ever be tired of Bath?" (Jane Austen)

An 18th-century tower (above) looks down from Fish Hill. Tranquillity at St John's Lock, Lechlade (left). Holland House (below) in Cropthorne. Old houses still remain in Dursley (opposite page, below left), contrasting with the grandeur of Gloucester Cathedral (opposite page, below right). Chedworth (opposite page, top) is particularly noted for its flowers, among them countless lilies of the valley, reputedly planted by the Romans. "I am the rose of Sharon, and the lily of the valleys." (Song of Solomon)

The spire of Salisbury Cathedral (top left) soars high above the Avon river. Stone monoliths (top right) at Avebury. A house in Herefordshire (right), chequered black and white, and dappled with sunshine and flowers. The town of Ledbury (above) has kept its lovely, old buildings. Seen here is cobbled Church Lane. Castle Combe (opposite page, below) is one of England's prettiest villages. Stonehenge (opposite page, top) stands majestic on Salisbury Plain and as the sun sets it silhouettes the vast stones, some of which weigh over twenty tons. "Now the sun is laid to sleep". (Ben Jonson)

Bournemouth (top left) is a popular resort on the Dorset coast. Shaftesbury (top right) was a fortified town in Saxon times. It overlooks the Blackmoor Vale and figures in the novels of Thomas Hardy under its old name of Shaston. The huge figure (above) cut into the hillside near Weymouth is called either the Osmington Man, or King George III. Not far from Lulworth lies the huge limestone arch (centre right) known as Durdle Door, which juts out into the sea. Edward I conferred the title 'Regis' on the town that is known as Lyme Regis today (right) when he took shelter in its bay during his wars with the French. The village of Corfe Castle (opposite) is dominated by its stark, spectacular fortress.

"I love all that thou lovest,
Spirit of Delight:
The fresh Earth in new leaves dressed,
And the starry night;
Autumn evening, and the morn
When the golden mists are born."

(P.B. Shelley)

Southampton (opposite page, top) has its origins deep in history. From here, in 1620, the Pilgrim Fathers set sail on the first leg of their epic journey. A glorious example of the English countryside is on the River Test, at Fullerton (opposite page, below). Parts of the original structure of Winchester Cathedral (below), which was commenced in 1079, can still be seen as well as the great Winchester Bible dating from the 12th century. The tiny village of Buckler's Hard (bottom) was once a great shipbuilding centre. The favourite ship of Admiral Lord Nelson, the *Agamemnon*, was built here in 1781. British warships were made from oak in those days, so it was quite logical to make use of this village, close to the New Forest where there was plenty of timber. Swan Green, Hampshire (left), is the setting for that most English of games – cricket.

"Our England is a garden,
and such gardens are not made
By singing:- 'Oh, how beautiful!' and
sitting in the shade".

(Rudyard Kipling)

Opposite page: (top left) Godshill, Isle of Wight and (below) Yarmouth. (Top right) Battle of the Flowers, Jersey. (Centre right) water-wheel on the Isle of Man. This page: (left) Creux Harbour, Sark. (Above) Freshwater Bay, Isle of Wight. (Top) La Corbière, Jersey. "Oh! what a snug little Island". (T. Dibdin)

Opposite page: (top left) Midhurst, West Sussex. (Top right) the Royal Pavilion, Brighton. (Centre left) the castle at Bodiam. (Centre right) Eastbourne. (Below left) Arundel Castle. (Below right) chalk cliffs at Birling Gap. This page, left, from top: Leeds Castle, Kent; Knole, a house dating from 1465; a ruined Norman castle at Tonbridge. (Left) Scotney Castle. (Above) traditional Kent oast houses converted into homes.

"The Stately Homes of England
How beautiful they stand".
(Noel Coward)

Mist envelops tree-lined fields in a Surrey valley (opposite page) near Dorking. The White Horse Inn, Dorking, (top left) is 400 years old and Charles Dickens once stayed here. The Angel Hotel, Guildford (left), possesses a coaching yard and an old wooden gallery. Hampton Court Palace (below) borders on the River Thames. Begun in 1514 by Cardinal Wolsey, it was the favourite country home of King Henry VIII. Five of his wives lived here and the ghosts of Jane Seymour and Catherine Howard roam there. The Chinese pagoda (above) in the Royal Botanic Gardens, Kew.

"Go down to Kew in lilac-time (it isn't far from London!)" (Alfred Noyes)

Londinium was founded on the north side of the River Thames by the Roman invader. Today, the river is flanked by jetties, wharves and docks, as well as numerous historic buildings, and is spanned by several graceful bridges. The dome of St Paul's Cathedral rises high on the skyline and Tower Bridge (above) has a dream-like quality in the pink light of dawn.

"Every drop of the Thames is liquid history." (J. Burns)

Parks and greens (left) mingle among the pillars of London's skyline. (Right) The National Westminster tower – 600 feet high with 52 floors. The dome of St Paul's Cathedral dominates the riverside (above, top right and opposite page, below right). Westminster Abbey (opposite page, top and below left) is filled with tombs and memorials of Britain's rulers and heroes.

"Westminster Abbey or victory!" (Horatio Nelson)

London is a tapestry of historic treasures, loved by the tourist. Opposite page: (top) lovely St James's Park with Buckingham Palace reflected in its waters. (Below right) a soldier in one of the Guards' regiments wearing the traditional bearskin. (Below left) the White Tower, William the Conqueror's London fortress. This page: (far right) Nelson's Column and Trafalgar Square. (Right and above) the Clock Tower and Houses of Parliament, famous throughout the world.

"England is the mother of Parliaments."
(John Bright)

London's lush greenery in its many parks and gardens provides an oasis of peace and tranquillity. The bandstand (top) in St James's Park. Landseer's lions on a misty morning (above) in Trafalgar Square. Piccadilly Circus (left) is one of London's landmarks with its bright lights appeal.

"Good-bye, Piccadilly, farewell, Leicester Square,
It's a long, long way to Tipperary, but my heart's right there!" (Williams and Judge)

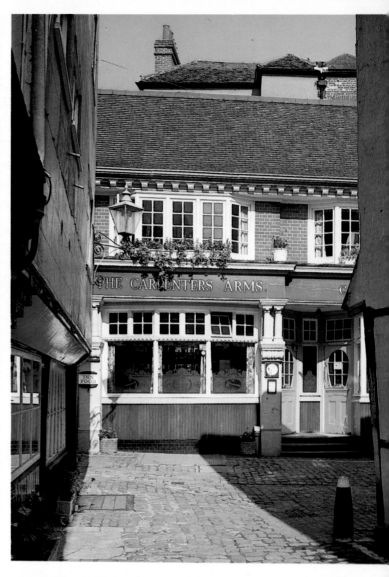

Opposite page: dominated by its royal
and magnificent castle, the Victorian
town of Windsor is a delight to behold.
This page: Blenheim Palace (top) is the
celebrated birthplace of Sir Winston
Churchill. Boats (left) moored at the
old mill, Hambledon and (above) in
Boulters Lock. "There is nothing...half
so much worth doing as simply messing
about in boats." (Kenneth Grahame)

This page: (top) the Thames at Henley;
(above) at Oxford and (right) Goring lock.
Opposite page: Oxford, famous seat of
learning. (Top) Christ Church College,
founded by Cardinal Wolsey in 1525; (below
left) Magdalen College; (below right) the
Radcliffe Camera.

"I saw the spires of Oxford
As I was passing by,
The gray spires of Oxford
Against a pearl-gray sky." (W. Letts)

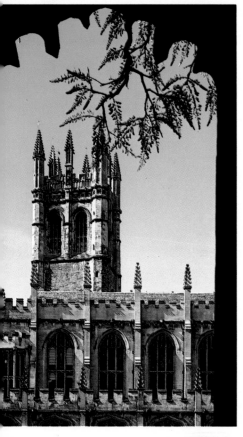

Opposite page: (top left) Norwich Cathedral; (top right) in Walsham le Willows; (centre right) sailing boats moored at Potter Heigham; (below left) Guildhall, Lavenham; (below right) Cavendish. This page: (left) remains of the ruined Cluniac Priory, Castle Acre; (below) Blickling Hall, begun in 1616; (above and below left) winds from the North Sea gave windmills their power. Betjeman in 'East Anglian Bathe':

"To see the whistling bent-grass on the leeside
And then the tumbled breaker-line appear".

Opposite page: (top) the American Cemetery in Cambridgeshire. (Below) Lincoln Cathedral, which contains the best of the four copies of the Magna Carta. This page: the University of Cambridge was established early in the 13th century. (Above) Christ's College; (right) Trinity Hall, founded in 1350 by the Bishop of Norwich. Ely Cathedral (far right), begun in 1083, is a demonstration of magnificent architecture. (Top) a punt makes its graceful way, past stately buildings, along the River Cam. "If you don't like my story get out of the punt." (James Joyce)

St Mary's Church (top), Warwick, stands over this town on the banks of the River Avon and is well known for its 15th century Beauchamp Chapel. Stratford is a living memorial to William Shakespeare. The Royal Shakespeare Theatre (above); the beautiful parish church of Holy Trinity (right) is the Bard's burial place and (opposite page) Anne Hathaway's Cottage in Shottery is the birthplace of the poet's wife. When he died in 1616, part of his last will and testament read: "Item, I give unto my wife my second best bed, with the furniture"!

Lock on the Grand Union Canal (top left) at Braunston, Northamptonshire. Wootton Hall (above) at Wootton Wawen. Thatched roof (left) in the village of Welford-on-Avon. Opposite page: (below left) Castleton, magnificently sited in the Peak District. (Top) Packwood House and its yew tree garden (below right).

"What of the bow?
The bow was made in England:
Of true wood, of yew-wood,
The wood of English bows."
(Conan Doyle)

Bramhall Hall (top) dates from the 16th century and is recognised as one of the finest examples in this country of half-timbered houses. Liverpool's famous dockside frontage (above) extends seven miles along the Mersey estuary and is dominated by the two towers of the Royal Liver Building with its legendary "Liver" birds. The Anglican Cathedral (right) was begun in 1904, after the design of Sir Giles Gilbert Scott. Opposite page: (top left and top right) above its famous promenade, the 518 ft Blackpool Tower stands serenely and each autumn there are the illuminations to see. (Below left) Chester's lovely sandstone cathedral was designed originally as a Benedictine Abbey. (Below right) stained glass in the Roman Catholic Metropolitan Cathedral, Liverpool.

"And life is colour and warmth and light
And a striving evermore for these".
(Julian Grenfell)

The peace and glorious beauty of the Lake District. Opposite page: Watendlath lies south of Derwent Water and was the setting for Sir Hugh Walpole's novel 'Rogue Herries'. Buttermere (top left); Crummock Water (centre left); Langdale Pikes (below left); Elterwater (top right) and Tarn Hows (above).

"A flock of sheep that leisurely pass by,
One after one; the sound of rain, and bees
Murmuring; the fall of rivers, winds and seas,
Smooth fields, white sheets of water, and pure sky". (Wordsworth)

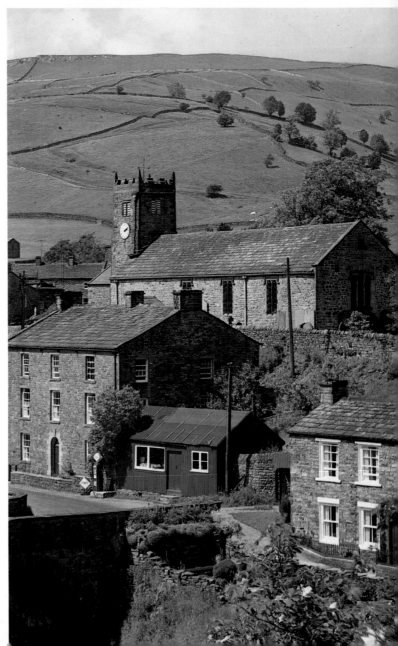

Opposite page: (top) the River Bain winds through Bainbridge and across the Yorkshire countryside; (below) Whitby on the North Yorkshire coast. This page: (top left) Durham Cathedral; (top right) the castle on Lindisfarne; (centre left) Knaresborough; (right) the village of Muker; (above) the ruins of Whitby Abbey.

"A ruin – yet what ruin! from its mass
Walls, palaces, half-cities, have been rear'd." (Lord Byron)

Opposite page: (left) Scottish piper; (top right) the busy harbour of Pittenween; (below right) a sky the colour of heather envelops the cliffs on the Isle of Mull. This page: (top left) the cantilevered Forth Railway Bridge carries trains from Edinburgh and the Lowlands. (Above) Callander is a popular resort and touring centre for the Trossachs. (Centre left) The Royal and Ancient Golf Club of St Andrews was founded in 1754. Shown here is the famous Road Hole, the seventeenth, on the Old Course. (Below left) the charming fishing and craft community of Plockton. (Below right) Crinan harbour on the Sound of Jura provides an ideal and idyllic centre for yachting.

"Land of brown heath and shaggy wood;Land of the mountain and the flood!"

(Sir Walter Scott)

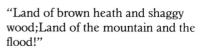

Snow covers the banks of Loch Leven (top left). A golden, misty sunset over sylvan Loch Laggan (above). The great sea loch (left) of Loch Etive with its impressive glen, through which flows a winding, lonely river. (Centre left) the climbers' hut in Glencoe, overshadowed by the brooding heights of the twin Buchaille Etive peaks. (Top right) the cascading Glencoe river winds through the pass, while the massif looks down on the moors where the Macdonalds were treacherously slaughtered. Opposite page: (below) an artist finds inspiration at tree-lined Loch Ard. (Top) the Cuillins of Skye with serrated peaks and wild corries.

"Sing me a song of a lad that is gone,
Say, could that lad be I?
Merry of soul he sailed on a day
Over the sea to Skye." (R.L. Stevenson)

Eilean Donnan Castle (top) is now a museum and clan war memorial. (Above) Dunbeath Castle, south of Dunbeath. Imposing Inverness Castle (right). Opposite page: (top left) Inveraray Castle. (Top right) Castle Stalker, Appin. (Centre right) Elgin Cathedral. (Below) Lochranza Castle, Isle of Arran. (Centre left) Stirling Castle overlooks the bloody battlefield of Bannockburn.

"Scots, wha hae wi' Wallace bled,
Scots, wham Bruce has often led,
Welcome to your gory bed,
Or to glorious victory!" (R. Burns)

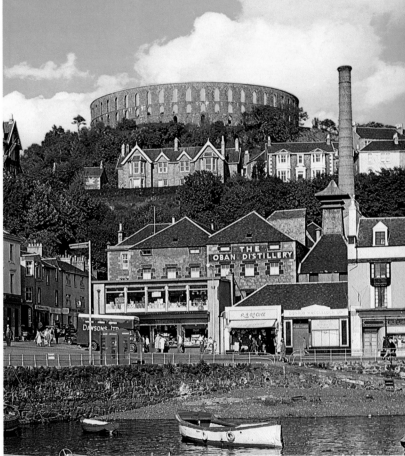

"When Britain first, at Heaven's command,
Arose from out the azure main,
This was the charter of the land,
And guardian angels sung this strain:
'Rule, Britannia, rule the waves;
Britons never will be slaves.'"

(James Thomson)

"There are no countries in the world less known by the British than these selfsame British Islands."

(George Borrow)

Copyright ©1988 by Colour Library Books Ltd.,
Guildford, Surrey, England.
First published in USA 1988
by Exeter Books
Distributed by Bookthrift
Exeter is a trademark of Bookthrift Marketing, Inc.
Bookthrift is a registered trademark of Bookthrift Marketing, Inc.
New York, New York

ISBN 0–671–06904–7

Printed in Spain by Cronion, S.A.

# DATE DUE

| | | | |
|---|---|---|---|
| | | | |
| | | | |
| | | | |
| | | | |
| | | | |
| | | | |
| | | | |
| | | | |
| | | | |
| | | | |
| | | | |
| | | | |
| | | | |
| | | | |
| | | | |
| | | | |
| | | | |
| | | | |
| | | | |

Demco, Inc. 38-293